Transformational You!

Create the change you want to see!

31 Power Statements & Affirmations to Live By

A Journal of Reflections

Tina L. Greer

ISBN-13: 978-1530432714
ISBN-10:1530432715

DEDICATION

This book is dedicated to the entrepreneur that keeps pushing no matter the obstacles ahead. Never give up on your goals and dreams.

ACKNOWLEDGMENTS

I want to thank my family and friends who believed in me; from the little girl who lived in the projects, to now a successful entrepreneur. You all have blessed me with your kind words and assistance in my journey. I would not be where I am today without your love and support.

CONTENTS

Introduction

Power Statement (1)   I am Built for This!

Power Statement (2)   I am making Boss Moves!

Power Statement (3)   I will leave a legacy of love & prosperity for generations to come!

Power Statement (4)   I am Worthy!

Power Statement (5)   Keep Pushing!

Power Statement (6)   Greatness lives within me!

Power Statement (7)   Keep Fighting!

Power Statement (8)   I am my Sister's & Brother's Keeper.

Power Statement (9)   Discovery begins when I open my mind to limitless opportunities!

Power Statement (10)   I am walking in my Purpose!

Power Statement (11)   I am Beautiful!

Power Statement (12)   My Smile is Sexy.

Power Statement (13)   My Eyes are the Gateway to my Soul.

Power Statement (14)   I enter a crowded room with Grace & Style.

Power Statement (15)   Watch me Grow!

Power Statement (16)   Watch me Prosper!

Power Statement (17)   I am a Solutions Provider.

Power Statement (18)   I am a Cash Flow Magnet; Money is constantly flowing my way.

Power Statement (19)   I am the ultimate Coin Collector!

Power Statement (20)   I Give out of Abundance.

Power Statement (21)   I am Unbreakable, I am an Overcomer!

Power Statement (22)   I am a Servant Leader.

Power Statement (23)   Stop the Clock; I am taking time out for me!

Power Statement (24)   Quitters never win and contentment never moves, keep growing into your destiny!

Power Statement (25)   Keep the Sparkle in Your Eyes & Passion in Your Soul.

Power Statement (26)   Self-Care is Self-Love.

Power Statement (27)   I will be the Change I want to See.

Power Statement (28)   I will make a difference; I will show up for Success!

Power Statement (29)   My Health is my Wealth!

Power Statement (30)   Transformational You! I will transform my mind, body, and business!

Power Statement (31)   My words are a two edged sword. I can choose to uplift or choose to knock down. I choose to Empower!

Summary

About the Author

INTRODUCTION

This journal of reflections was designed to awaken your dreams and goals to achieve success in business and life. It also reminds you that you are better than your circumstances.

Read each power statement out loud and answer the questions provided. This will help you in your journey to be the change you want to see!

Power Statement (1)

I am Built for This!

Describe how you have faced your obstacles and turned a bad situation into success.

_____

_____

_____

_____

_____

_____

_____

_____

_____

_____

Power Statement (2)

I am making Boss Moves!

Explain how your brand image and expertise sealed the deal in closing a sale for you.

_____

_____

_____

_____

_____

_____

_____

_____

_____

_____

_____

_____

_____

_____

_____

_____

_____

_____

_____

_____

_____

_____

_____

_____

_____

_____

_____

_____

_____

Power Statement (3)

I will leave a legacy of love & prosperity for generations to come!

Describe what plans or processes you have or will put in place to change or enhance your family tree. How will you foster generational wealth?

_____

_____

_____

_____

_____

_____

_____

_____

_____

Power Statement (4)

I am Worthy!

Identify ways you believe you are worthy of all that is good and kind; and express the reasons why you are special in your own right and that you know you were placed here on earth for a reason.

_____

_____

_____

_____

_____

_____

_____

_____

Power Statement (5)

Keep Pushing!

Don't give up - you are on the cusp of your breakthrough! Amidst all of the obstacles you face on a daily basis, identify the reasons why you should continue to move forward.

_____

_____

_____

_____

_____

_____

_____

_____

_____

_____

_____

_____

_____

_____

_____

_____

_____

_____

_____

_____

_____

_____

_____

_____

_____

_____

_____

_____

_____

_____

Power Statement (6)

Greatness lives within me!

You are destined for greatness! You have qualities of kings and queens. You are royalty! What ideas have you thought about throughout the years and just have never acted upon them? Write those dreams and desires down. Put it out there into the atmosphere.

_____

_____

_____

_____

_____

_____

_____

_____

_____

Power Statement (7)

Keep Fighting!

Nobody said the road would be easy. Anything worth having is worth fighting for! Write down the people, milestones, or possessions that you are so passionate about that you would not let go.

_____

_____

_____

_____

_____

_____

_____

_____

_____

_____

Power Statement (8)

I am my Sister's & Brother's Keeper.

No one left behind. Explain how others have supported you in your journey to achieve success. Identify them by name.

_____

_____

_____

_____

_____

_____

_____

_____

_____

_____

_____

_____

_____

_____

_____

_____

_____

_____

_____

_____

_____

_____

_____

_____

_____

_____

_____

_____

_____

Power Statement (9)

Discovery begins when I open my mind to limitless opportunities!

Never stop dreaming or exploring the world. How have you been able to think outside of the box and grow into your greatness?

_____

_____

_____

_____

_____

_____

_____

_____

Power Statement (10)

I am walking in my Purpose!

A purpose walk is steady and has a flow. You may have obstacles; however, you are willing to fight to overcome them. Identify how you are walking into your purpose.

_____

_____

_____

_____

_____

_____

_____

_____

_____

Power Statement (11)

I am Beautiful!

You must first love yourself before you can love anyone else. Describe the ways you feel beautiful.

_____

_____

_____

_____

_____

_____

_____

_____

_____

_____

_____

Power Statement (12)

My Smile is Sexy.

Explain how you light up a room when you smile.

_____

_____

_____

_____

_____

_____

_____

_____

_____

_____

_____

Power Statement (13)

My Eyes are the Gateway to my Soul.

God, allow me to see what you want me to see. I want to manifest the gifts and talents you have given me so the world can see what I have through you. Share your deepest thoughts.

_____

_____

_____

_____

_____

_____

_____

_____

_____

_____

Power Statement (14)

I enter a crowded room with Grace and Style.

Identify how you are able to maintain your professional image through your attire and attitude while closing the sale. Why should they buy from you?

_____

_____

_____

_____

_____

_____

_____

_____

_____

Power Statement (15)

Watch me Grow!

Explain how personal development has helped you grow as a person.

_____

_____

_____

_____

_____

_____

_____

_____

_____

_____

Power Statement (16)

Watch me Prosper!

You should have at least 7 streams of income. Identify ways you will create multiple streams of income and list your 7 streams.

_____

_____

_____

_____

_____

_____

_____

_____

_____

_____

_____

_____

Power Statement (17)

I am a Solutions Provider.

What separates you from the rest? What is your unique identifier? Why do people want to do business with you?

_____

_____

_____

_____

_____

_____

_____

_____

_____

_____

Power Statement (18)

I am a Cash Flow Magnet; Money is constantly flowing my way.

Explain how you are closing sales and cashing checks.

_____

_____

_____

_____

_____

_____

_____

_____

_____

_____

Power Statement (19)

I am the ultimate Coin Collector!

Where are my Rich Friends…Identify the systems you use to monitor your business and how it has helped you streamline processes.

_____

_____

_____

_____

_____

_____

_____

_____

_____

Power Statement (20)

I Give out of Abundance.

Explain how you have been able to bless others with your overflow.

_____

_____

_____

_____

_____

_____

_____

_____

_____

_____

_____

Power Statement (21)

I am Unbreakable, I am an Overcomer!

You are a person that does not give up easily; your test has become your testimony! How have you used this source of power to help others?

_____

_____

_____

_____

_____

_____

_____

_____

_____

Power Statement (22)

I am a Servant Leader.

Explain how you help others achieve their desired success. How does that make you feel in providing a service to others?

_____

_____

_____

_____

_____

_____

_____

_____

_____

_____

Power Statement (23)

Stop the Clock; I am taking time out for me!

Identify ways to love yourself. What does self-care mean to you?

_____

_____

_____

_____

_____

_____

_____

_____

_____

_____

Power Statement (24)

Quitters never win and contentment never moves, keep growing into your destiny!

What are you doing on a daily basis to stretch your mind and your vision for your life?

_____

_____

_____

_____

_____

_____

_____

_____

Power Statement (25)

Keep the Sparkle in Your Eyes & Passion in Your Soul.

You are beautiful and wonderfully made. You shine bright with your beauty and smile. How do you express this love to others in your daily walk?

_____

_____

_____

_____

_____

_____

_____

_____

_____

_____

Power Statement (26)

Self-Care is Self-Love.

What activities do you participate in to show love for your body, mind, & soul?

_____

_____

_____

_____

_____

_____

_____

_____

_____

_____

Power Statement (27)

I will be the Change I want to See.

If it has to be, it is up to me. You are not an island; however, you must make the first move. Identify ways you are going to move forward to achieve your goals.

_____

_____

_____

_____

_____

_____

_____

_____

_____

_____

Power Statement (28)

I will make a difference; I will show up for Success!

Success leaves clues. Identify mentors that have helped you along your journey to achieve success. What tips and strategies have they shared with you?

_____

_____

_____

_____

_____

_____

_____

_____

_____

_____

Power Statement (29)

My Health is my Wealth!

Identify what programs you are following to obtain maximum wellness. How do you relieve stress? How does it make you feel?

_____

_____

_____

_____

_____

_____

_____

_____

_____

_____

_____

Power Statement (30)

Transformational You! I will transform my mind, body, and business!

What steps are you taking to change the trajectory of your mind, body, and business to become wildly successful? What are your financial goals for this year?

_____

_____

_____

_____

_____

_____

_____

_____

_____

_____

_____

_____

_____

_____

_____

_____

_____

_____

_____

_____

_____

_____

_____

_____

_____

_____

_____

_____

_____

_____

_____

Power Statement (31)

My words are a two edged sword. I can choose to uplift or choose to knock down. I choose to Empower!

Write down affirmations and words of encouragement that inspire you.

_____

_____

_____

_____

_____

_____

_____

_____

_____

SUMMARY

Use these power statements/affirmations to constantly remind yourself that you are destined to achieve greatness! Continue to feed your intellect, grow, and transform your mind, body and business!

ABOUT THE AUTHOR

 Tina Greer is a native of Illinois, military spouse of retired Army Sergeant 1st Class, and been afforded the opportunity to live abroad in Japan and across the United States. She has always aspired to help others in the business arena, but at the time she did not know what area she wanted to focus on. Through helping many colleagues, friends, and clients with advice on how to grow their respective businesses, she decided to specialize in business coaching specifically women entrepreneurs from start-up to five years in business.

Coupled with her educational background, Master of Public Administration (MPA) specializing in finance, and her expertise of working in corporate America for twenty plus years with the last ten years specializing in business strategy and pricing for a multi-million dollar company, she is able to assist aspiring entrepreneurs and small business owners in creating sustainable robust businesses.

She does this by providing business coaching and consulting services; teaching the fundamentals of business, and positioning business owners for profits from the initial goal setting to closing the deal. She also provides customized coaching programs strategizing various ways to create additional streams of income. One of the popular coaching programs is the Writer's Workshop where we successfully help you write and publish your first book.

Greer Business Solutions coaching programs are available in person and online. We also provide group coaching as well as 1-1 coaching.

Tina Greer is also a professional speaker focusing on topics such as leadership, networking with impact, sisterhood, and inspirational messages. For bookings inquiries, email info@tinagreer.com.

Our focus is to help others succeed in business and in life by identifying their passion and purpose, cultivating it into a sustainable financial lifestyle!

GREER BUSINESS SOLUTIONS

Website: www.tinagreer.com

Email: info@tinagreer.com

Follow me on Twitter & Periscope @LT_Millionaire

Facebook: www.facebook.com/greerbusinesssolutions

www.ingramcontent.com/pod-product-compliance
Lightning Source LLC
Chambersburg PA
CBHW060417190526
45169CB00002B/939